# Fact Frenzy™

.com

WRITTEN BY

## JAWN GROSS

ISBN: 0692654127
ISBN-13: 978-0692654125

Choose the letter of the correct answer. Each question has only one answer that is correct. There are questions from a wide range of subjects. Some are easy, some are hard. Some are tricky, some are ridiculous. See how well you did according to the answer key in the back of the book. Good luck!

1. In order to camouflage themselves, _____ allow algae to grow on their hair.

    a. butterflies

    b. sloths

    c. catfish

    d. pandas

    e. tourists

2. It takes an average of 2,000 steps for a human to walk _____ .

    a. backwards

    b. to the bathroom

    c. one mile

    d. while texting

    e. on sunshine

3. The first American "storefront" movie theater opened in 1896, in the city of _____ .
   a. New Orleans
   b. Hollywood
   c. Omaha
   d. New York City
   e. Springfield

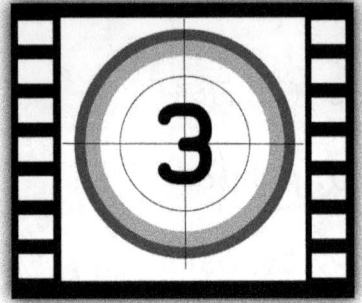

4. What percentage of Americans eat dinner while watching TV?
   a. 20%
   b. 70%
   c. 110%
   d. 40%
   e. 0%

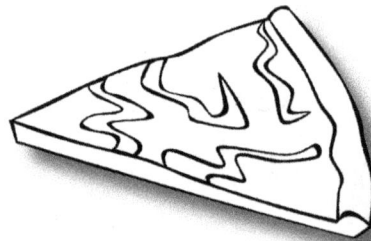

5. A carpenter from Denmark started a toy company in the 1930's. It was called _____ , which means "play well."

   a. Tinker Toys
   b. Lego
   c. Lincoln Logs
   d. K'NEX
   e. Play Well

6. Kazakhstan, Canada, Australia and Niger are the largest producers of _____ , the ore that is mined to make nuclear energy.

   a. sugar
   b. radishes
   c. plutonium
   d. uranium
   e. kryptonite

7. A community that includes living and non-living things is called _____ .

a. an ecosystem

b. organic diversity

c. erosion

d. atmospheric particles

e. gas station food

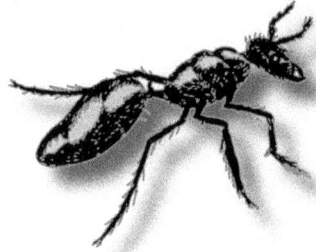

8. The Supreme Court of the United States is part of which branch of government?

a. Legislative.

b. Experimental.

c. Executive.

d. Judicial.

e. Temperamental.

9. "Lunacy" is an ancient myth that draws a connection between mania and _____.

  a. country music
  b. planet alignment
  c. seasons
  d. moon cycles
  e. Pop Rocks

10. The Chinese first developed soy bean curd, which the Japanese later called _____.

  a. oden
  b. gyoza
  c. tofu
  d. wagashi
  e. lunch

11. Penn State University's mascot is the _____ .
   a. Trojan Horse
   b. Nittany Lion
   c. Dueling Banjos
   d. Bobcat
   e. Sabertooth

12. John Garnet Carter, in 1927, was the first to patent _____ .
   a. hide and seek
   b. tennis
   c. dodge ball
   d. miniature golf
   e. mashed potatoes

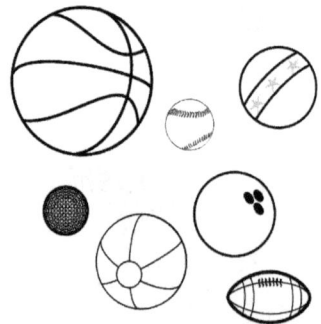

13. When does a funnel cloud officially become a tornado?
   a. When it starts to spin.
   b. When it touches the ground.
   c. When it picks up a cow.
   d. When it gets a name.
   e. When people yell, "there's a tornado!"

14. Sometimes, vultures can't fly because _____.
   a. they forget how
   b. they just ate a lot
   c. walking is cheaper
   d. of no-fly zones
   e. there is a land battle with the crows

15. The internet was first invented in the 1960's by the U.S Department of Defense through a project called _____ .

   a. ARPANET
   b. WORLD WIDE WEB
   c. WESCAC
   d. SKYNET
   e. NCIS

16. The first human organ was successfully transplanted in 1954. It was _____ .

   a. a kidney
   b. a heart
   c. a brain
   d. a liver
   e. chest hair

17. Disney's first animated feature film was in 1937. It was _____ .

   a. Steamboat Mickey
   b. Cinderella
   c. Snow White and the 7 Dwarfs
   d. Shrek
   e. Poltergeist

18. Miguel Hidalgo y Costilla was a leader of the Mexican War of Independence and was nicknamed "el Zorro." His occupation was a _____ .

   a. priest
   b. blacksmith
   c. soldier
   d. farmer
   e. dance instructor

19. Chewing ice is sometimes linked to a disorder known as _____.
   a. hydrophobia
   b. pica
   c. chew-chew
   d. hypochondria
   e. caulrophobia

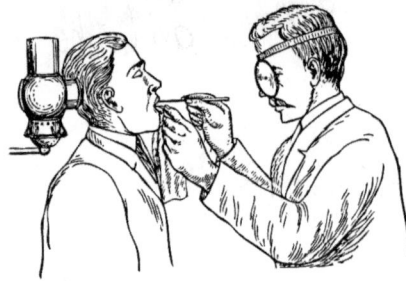

20. The first space probe to take close-up photos of Uranus and Neptune was _____.
   a. Sputnik 1
   b. Voyager 2
   c. Rover 3
   d. Helios 4
   e. Space Ghost

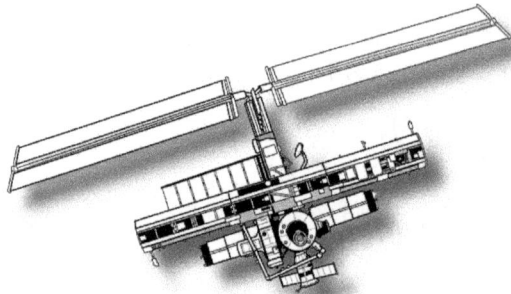

21. The Statue of Liberty is green due to _____ .

a. the weathering of its copper

b. solar panels

c. green paint

d. chlorophyll

e. envy

22. The bison is the official state animal of which three states?

a. Ohio, Pennsylvania, and Maine.

b. Texas, California, and Connecticut.

c. Nebraska, Tennessee, and Oregon.

d. Kansas, Oklahoma, and Wyoming.

e. Flux, chaos, and euphoria.

23. Thunder is heard moments after lightning is seen because _____ .

   a. it's how the spirits communicate

   b. the speed of sound is slower than the speed of light

   c. the angels threw a gutter ball

   d. the universe is expanding

   e. lightning is choosing its next target

24. The movement of energy through substances in longitudinal waves would best describe _____ .

   a. potential energy

   b. hydraulic displacement

   c. sound energy

   d. photonic length

   e. the neutron dance

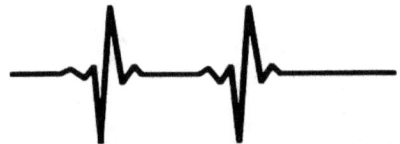

25. Switzerland and Vatican City are the only countries that have _____ flags.

   a. square
   b. circular
   c. red
   d. pledge to the
   e. zero

26. In 1869, the transcontinental railroad was a major development because it moved people _____.

   a. around the world
   b. to Canada
   c. to work and back
   d. westward
   e. to start singing

27. Electrical energy is _____ .

   a. the movement of electrons

   b. the vibration of metal

   c. seen by cats

   d. created by stationary objects

   e. wizardry

28. The largest purely terrestrial Antarctic animal is a _____ .

   a. penguin

   b. wingless fly

   c. seal

   d. polar bear

   e. yeti

29. The first NASA space shuttle test flight was on August 12, 1977. The shuttle's name was _____ .

    a. Columbia
    b. Challenger
    c. Enterprise
    d. Atlantis
    e. Serenity

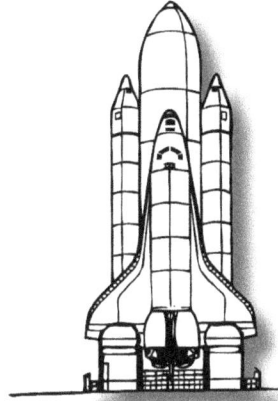

30. On July 10th, 1973, _____ became free from British rule and became a sovereign nation.

    a. Indonesia
    b. The Bahamas
    c. Scotland
    d. Asia
    e. the Beatles

31. It is a Ukrainian tradition to decorate Christmas trees with _____

    a. spider webs
    b. peppers
    c. licorice
    d. oregano
    e. catnip

32. The creator of Star Trek was _____.

    a. George Lucas
    b. C.S. Lewis
    c. Gene Roddenberry
    d. Isaac Asimov
    e. David Hasselhoff

33. The first city in the world to have a population of one million people was _____.
   a. Rome, Italy
   b. New York, NY
   c. Erie, PA
   d. London, England
   e. Motown

34. The first African American woman to anchor Nashville's WVTF-TV — at the age of only 19 — was ___.
   a. Janet Jackson
   b. Oprah Winfrey
   c. Tyra Banks
   d. Diana Ross
   e. Mabel "Madea" Simmons

35. In the movie "Selma," Dr. Martin Luther King Jr. was played by _____.
   a. Levar Burton
   b. David Oyelowo
   c. Will Smith
   d. Tyler Perry
   e. Matthew Broderick

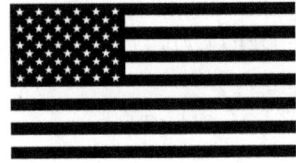

36. Foxes use _____ to help them hunt for prey.
   a. the earth's magnetic field
   b. sonar
   c. plastic ducks
   d. tips from Field & Stream
   e. questionable interrogation tactics

37. During the time of American pioneers, the first covered wagons were built during the _____ .
 a. late 1800's
 b. battle of Armageddon
 c. early 1700'S
 d. building of the pyramids
 e. hippy revolution

38. The famous "HOLLYWOOD" sign, built in 1923 in Los Angeles, California, originally was spelled _____ .
 a. Hollyworld
 b. Hollywoodland
 c. backwards
 d. Bollywood
 e. Hollaback

39. "As you were" is a military command that means to resume your previous activities, after _____ .

   a. a three mile run

   b. 30 pushups

   c. breakfast

   d. standing at attention to salute an officer

   e. a few knock-knock jokes

40. Fleas can jump 110 times their own height --- the equivalent to a human jumping over _____ .

   a. a 30-story building

   b. the Grand Canyon

   c. the moon

   d. a candlestick

   e. parallel dimensions

41. A type of penguin that has light orange marks on its head and chest is the _____ .
   a. Gentoo Penguin
   b. Adélie Penguin
   c. Chinstrap Penguin
   d. King Penguin
   e. Devito Penguin

42. On June 14, 1777, the adoption of _____ became official in the United States.
   a. the American flag
   b. cursive writing
   c. the metric system
   d. the National Anthem
   e. disco

43. Only 1% of the human population is equally adept at using both left and right hands without having a dominant hand. This is known as _____.

    a. magic
    b. ambidexterity
    c. hand jive
    d. symmetric bioelectricity
    e. miming

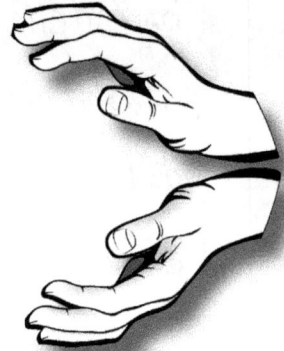

44. Root beer was originally made using the roots from _____.

    a. raspberry bushes
    b. maple trees
    c. ginger
    d. sassafras trees
    e. family trees

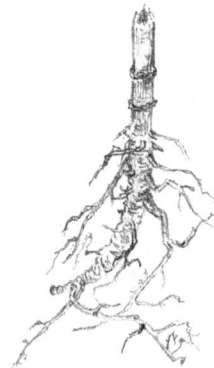

45. The name of the bell in London's famous clock tower is _____.

   a. Winchester
   b. Big Boss
   c. Big Ben
   d. the Liberty Bell
   e. Clarabell

46. Kobe Bryant's parents named him after the famous _____ of Kobe, Japan.

   a. river
   b. naval ship
   c. beef
   d. community theatre
   e. talking dolphin

47. Salmon migrate from the ocean to the rivers they came from to spawn. After which, they _____ .

   a. turn pink

   b. die

   c. grow legs

   d. migrate south

   e. part on good terms

48. The three branches of government in the United States are _____ .

   a. executive, legislative, and judicial

   b. federal, local, and state

   c. federal, commonwealth, and magistrate

   d. presidential, congressional, and municipal

   e. empirical, jedi, and sith

49. Sharks have a small, thick piece of cartilage called a basihyal. It is mostly useless to most sharks. But it is otherwise known as a _____ .

a. nose

b. brain

c. vocal cord

d. tongue

e. sign to scream for help

50. A honey bee flaps its wings _____ .

a. 230 times per second

b. over 1,000,000 times per second

c. only when it is flying

d. only when it is happy

e. to the tune of "Flight of the Bumblebee" when no one is around

51. The official state exercise in Missouri is _____ .

a. crunches

b. chin ups

c. jumping jacks

d. running

e. criss-cross applesauce

52. Scalene, equilateral, and isosceles are different types of _____ .

a. quadrilaterals

b. triangles

c. hexagons

d. octagons

e. moisturizers

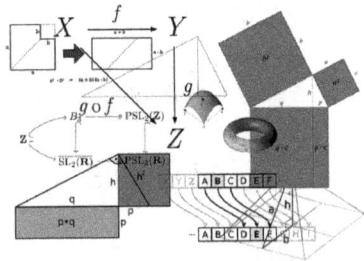

53. Although most land animals can, _____ and _____ cannot walk backwards.

  a. kangaroos and emus
  b. elephants and hippos
  c. ferrets and aardvarks
  d. turtles and tortoises
  e. zombies and bull runners

54. How much does a peck of pickled peppers weigh?
  a. A hogs head.
  b. 10 to 14 pounds.
  c. 1.3 metric tons.
  d. 36 quarts.
  e. A plethora of puppies.

55. In a black hole, the "point of no return" refers to the _____.

   a. string theory
   b. dark matter
   c. event horizon
   d. acid relflux
   e. empty gas tank

56. The name of the Sesame Street actress who is Deaf and taught American Sign Language is _____.

   a. Linda Bove
   b. Marlee Matlin
   c. Deanne Bray
   d. Phyllis Frelich
   e. Super Grover

57. North Korea has the largest _____ in the world.

    a. aquarium

    b. stadium

    c. military

    d. Starbucks

    e. Bill of Rights

58. Though not always noticeable, iguanas have a third _____ .

    a. kidney

    b. tail

    c. eye

    d. name

    e. cousin

59. In 1965, the Voting Rights Act was signed into law by president Lyndon B. Johnson, making it illegal to _____ .
   a. vote more than once in the same election
   b. deny the right to vote based on race
   c. gamble on election outcomes
   d. run for any office if you were born in Canada
   e. disagree with the president

60. "Two," "to" and "too" are examples of _____ .
   a. homophones
   b. homographs
   c. hieroglyphics
   d. haiku
   e. Takei

61. C.S. Lewis wrote the novel, "The Lion, the Witch and the Wardrobe," which was part of a seven-book series called, _____ .

    a. The Adventures of Aslan
    b. Tales from Narnia
    c. The Chronicles of Narnia
    d. The Lion's Tales
    e. Those Meddling Kids

62. The nucleus of _____ was discovered by Ernest Rutherford in 1911.

    a. molecules
    b. cells
    c. corks
    d. atoms
    e. pimples

63. Bubble tea, which is also called boba milk tea, was invented in _____ during the 1980's.

    a. Taiwan

    b. Japan

    c. China

    d. Russia

    e. McDonald's

64. Bruce Lee was born in _____ .

    a. Beijing, China

    b. Sao Paulo, Brazil

    c. St. Petersburg, Russia

    d. San Francisco, USA

    e. the world of illusion

65. Earth's orbit around the sun is in the shape of _____.

    a. a triangle

    b. an oval

    c. a circle

    d. a pyramid

    e. a snowflake

66. If the sun were to explode this instant, we wouldn't know for another _____.

    a. 80 years

    b. 800 days

    c. 8 minutes

    d. 8 seconds

    e. season finale

67. Birds are _____ blooded.

a. warm

b. cold

c. blue

d. green

e. hot

68. The mission of the SETI program, which analyzes radio signals from space, is to _____.

a. identify dark matter particles

b. search for extraterrestrial life

c. locate black holes

d. coordinate media satellite orbit

e. get free satellite radio

69. Even though it was part of Japanese culture for over 1,000 years, _____ didn't arrive in America until 1966.

   a. martial arts

   b. origami

   c. carp

   d. sushi

   e. samurais

70. Seagulls do have _____, but they really don't use them.

   a. taste buds

   b. central nervous systems

   c. feet

   d. noses

   e. table manners

71. The fastest land animal is the _____ .
    a. antelope
    b. greyhound
    c. cheetah
    d. coyote
    e. road runner

72. Sir Arthur Conan Doyle's fictional character, Sherlock Holmes, plays the _____ for his own enjoyment.
    a. bass guitar
    b. violin
    c. penny whistle
    d. bagpipes
    e. cowbell

73. At 4 months old, dogs begin to lose their
_____ .

    a. hearing
    b. baby teeth
    c. sense of smell
    d. sweat glands
    e. patience with mail carriers

74. Titanosaurs, which were dinosaurs that lived 100
millions years ago, were ____ .

    a. herbivores
    b. carnivores
    c. omnivores
    d. hunter-gatherers
    e. crazy about tacos

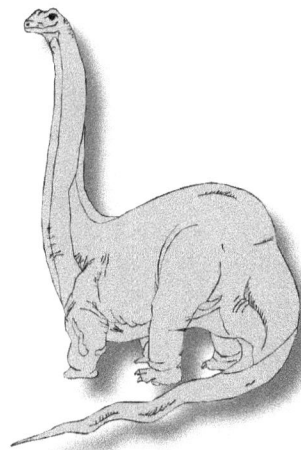

75. In the tall tale legend of Pecos Bill, his horse was named _____ .
    a. Gunslinger
    b. Windcatcher
    c. Princess
    d. Widowmaker
    e. Horsey

76. The Jungle Book was written in 1894 by English author _____ .
    a. Walt Disney
    b. J.K. Rowling
    c. Arthur Conan Doyle
    d. Rudyard Kipling
    e. Jack Handey

77. A large boulder on the edge of a cliff is an example of ____ .

   a. potential energy
   b. kinetic energy
   c. static energy
   d. electrical energy
   e. sheer energy

78. ____ , a Renaissance artist of the 15th century, is often credited as being the first to use oil paints.

   a. Leonardo da Vinci
   b. Salvador Dali
   c. Jan van Eyck
   d. Andy Worhol
   e. Bob Ross

79. The scientist who discovered the laws of motion and gravity was _____.
   a. Isaac Newton
   b. Albert Einstein
   c. Stephen Hawking
   d. Rosalind Franklin
   e. Bill Nye

80. The longest snake in the animal kingdom, which grows up to 35 feet (or, 10.668 meters), is the ___.
   a. anaconda
   b. king cobra
   c. reticulated python
   d. red-tailed boa
   e. plumber snake

81. A "Jacobson's organ" is located on the roof of snake's mouths. This organ is responsible for giving snakes an excellent sense of _____ .

   a. taste

   b. smell

   c. heat detection

   d. blood tracking

   e. humor

82. If you could fly around the earth's equator at the speed of light, you could _____ .

   a. go back in time

   b. pass the same point 7.5 times in one second

   c. meet people from other dimensions

   d. talk to whales

   e. wave to everyone on the smaller rides

83. The Chinese New Year festival traditionally lasts _____.

   a. a year
   b. a New York minute
   c. 23 days
   d. nine months
   e. until the Macy's parade ends

84. Cuba is the largest of the _____.

   a. British Isles
   b. Caribbean islands
   c. Jamaican islands
   d. plantain exporters
   e. cigar importers

85. Energy stored in the nucleus of an atom is an example of _____ .

a. cellular energy
b. nuclear energy
c. sound energy
d. kinetic energy
e. caffeine energy

86. Human-made sulfur dioxide and nitrogen oxide that falls to the earth during precipitation is commonly known as _____ .

a. acid rain
b. radioactive clouds
c. agricultural pollution
d. a sonic boom
e. thermal detonators

87. Which of the Marx brothers never appeared in any of the Marx Brothers' films?

a. Gummo.

b. Chico.

c. Harpo.

d. Zeppo.

e. Bambi.

88. Bowling was invented in _____ .

a. 1956

b. 1748

c. 1999

d. 3200 BC

e. someone's spare time

89. 0.9% of the earth's atmosphere is a gas known as _____.

   a. carbon dioxide

   b. nitrogen

   c. oxygen

   d. argon

   e. nitrous oxide

90. Crackers are made with _____, which prevent them from becoming too hard, and inhibits the formation of bubbles.

   a. square shapes

   b. holes

   c. salt

   d. care

   e. elf labor

91. The brightest star in the night sky, nicknamed "the Dog Star," is actually _____.
   a. Venus
   b. Andromeda
   c. Sirius
   d. Aquarius
   e. Duane Chapman

92. Composer Akira Ifukube created a technique of recording the sound of a resin-coated glove rubbing the string of a contrabass, and then slowing down the recording. This sound effect was used in movies as _____.
   a. light saber battles
   b. Godzilla's roar
   c. space ship explosions
   d. warp drive engines
   e. subliminal advertisement for popcorn

93. The 1964 Nobel Prize in Literature was awarded to _____, although he turned it down.

a. Shimon Peres
b. Jean-Paul Sartre
c. Jody Williams
d. Barak Obama
e. Larry the Cable Guy

94. Stanley Kubrick's 1968 film, with a popular music score of the same name composed by Alex North, was called _____.

a. 2001: A Space Odyssey
b. The Lost Boys
c. The Big Lebowski
d. Chariots of Fire
e. The Muppet Movie

95. The _____ can smell food up to 4 miles (7 km) away.

a. hammerhead shark
b. bluebottle fly
c. bottlenose dolphin
d. American indigo snake
e. Cookie Monster

96. Creating the 2nd longest-reigning British monarch, the United Kingdom of Great Britain and Ireland was ruled for 64 years by _____ .

a. Queen Anne
b. Queen Victoria
c. Queen Mary
d. Queen Elizabeth
e. Queen Latifa

97. In the tall tale legends of John Henry, he worked as a _____.

   a. politician

   b. inventor

   c. lumberjack

   d. railroad builder

   e. hand model

98. The creator of "Star Wars" was _____.

   a. Gene Roddenberry

   b. Steven Spielberg

   c. George Lucas

   d. Madeleine L'Engle

   e. Mel Brooks

Although leopards have a broad diet and are highly adaptable, they have been placed on the "near threatened" list due to hunting and killing by humans.

Steamboats were the primary means of water transportation in the early 1800's. Their top speed was generally 5 miles per hour.

99. In 1912, the largest ship ever built was 882 feet long and weighed 39,000 tons. It was the _____ .
   a. Ark
   b. USS Minnow
   c. Titanic
   d. Lollipop
   e. Yellow Submarine

100. U.S. Dollars are sometimes referred to as "bucks" because _____ used to be traded, before there was U.S. currency.
   a. deer skins
   b. moose antlers
   c. elk tails
   d. beaver teeth
   e. uncles

101. The book, "Little House on the Prairie" was written by _____ .

   a. Laura Ingalls Wilder
   b. Jane Austen
   c. Toni Morrison
   d. Sylvia Plath
   e. Agatha Christie

102. Setting a world record, in 2011 a company in England created a _____ weighing 6 tons. After the record was set, it was smashed apart so its pieces could be sold for charity.

   a. ceramic plate
   b. mirror
   c. chocolate bar
   d. coffin
   e. alarm clock

103. The first person to make a phone call to the moon was _____ .
   a. Alexander Graham Bell
   b. Richard Nixon
   c. Thomas Edison
   d. Claude Shannon
   e. a telemarketer

104. A creature that has between 5 to 15 rows of teeth would be _____ .
   a. kittens
   b. hyenas
   c. Komodo dragons
   d. sharks
   e. toddlers

105. A German chemist named Johann Wolfgang Döbereiner, invented his "Döbereiner's lamp" in 1816 --- otherwise known as the first _____ .

a. sparkler
b. lighter
c. lantern
d. wooden match
e. genie lamp

106. Chocolate comes from trees, while vanilla comes from _____ .

a. orchids
b. bushes
c. roots
d. minerals
e. candles

107. Scientists recently discovered bones from a type of extinct bird that was 6 feet and 6 inches (198 centimeters) and lived in Antarctica 40 million years ago. It is called the ____ .

a. arctic pterodactyl
b. colossus penguin
c. coldland owl
d. siberian parrot
e. buffalo chicken

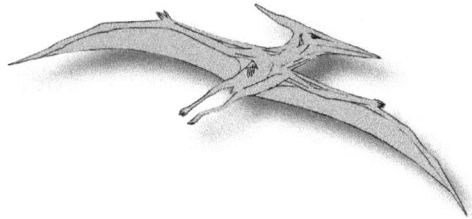

108. Some animals that live in the _____ have larger hearts and lungs to compensate for the lack of oxygen.

a. grasslands
b. rainforests
c. mountains
d. desert
e. Bronx

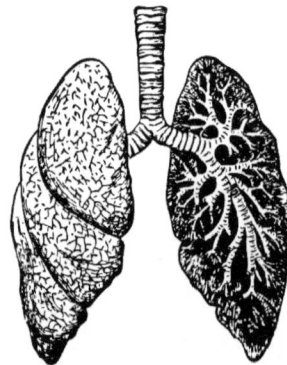

109. _____ actually prefer chocolate over cheese.

a. Mice
b. Beetles
c. Tropical fish
d. Frogs
e. People who are silly

110. A hot air balloon can only be manually steered in two directions, _____ .

a. left and right
b. forward and backward
c. up and down
d. northwest and southeast
e. upwind and downwind

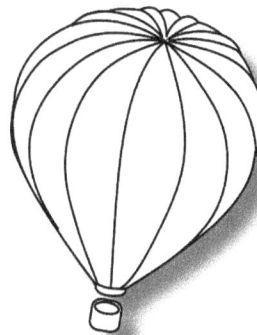

111. The first car that people could afford to buy in the 1910's was the _____ .
   a. Model T Ford
   b. Model A Ford.
   c. Model D Ford
   d. Studebaker
   e. Yugo

112. _____ divide roughly every 30 minutes.
   a. Bacteria
   b. Viruses
   c. Starfish
   d. Galaxies
   e. Math majors

113. The president of the United States is part of which branch of government?

   a. Legislative.

   b. Judicial.

   c. Executive.

   d. Central intelligence.

   e. Cowboy diplomacy.

114. In the United States, the Senate and the House of Representatives are part of which branch of government?

   a. Tormential.

   b. Legislative.

   c. Executive.

   d. Judicial.

   e. Clown college.

115. Horses were brought too the Americas in 1519 by explorers from _____ .

    a. the rains
    b. Spain
    c. Maine
    d. the plains
    e. Cleveland

116. Oil, gas, and coal are examples of _____ .

    a. prehistoric energy
    b. fossil fuels
    c. fracking
    d. biofuels
    e. renewable energy

117. The assassination of _____ drew most of Europe into World War 1.

   a. Archduke Franz Ferdinand
   b. Gavrilo Princip
   c. Abraham Lincoln
   d. Benito Mussolini
   e. Emperor Palpatine

118. The national animal of Scotland is the _____.

   a. lion
   b. eagle
   c. bear
   d. unicorn
   e. tribble

119. The biggest fish in the world, measuring 46 feet / 14 meters, are _____.

a. swordfish

b. catfish

c. beluga

d. whale sharks

e. mutant mermaids

120. The first known person to create and sell ___ was John Spilsbury, a London cartographer and engraver around 1760.

a. biscuits

b. pie crusts

c. ceramic mugs

d. sippie cups

e. jigsaw puzzles

121. There are _____ species of octopus in the world.

   a. 400 million

   b. 289

   c. 2

   d. 6 billion

   e. 8

122. The first _____ was published in Rome in 59 BC.

   a. trivia book

   b. newspaper

   c. theatre playbill

   d. sports card

   e. cook book

123. The _____ has been known to fly as high as 35,400 feet (10,800 m), and one actually crashed into an aircraft.

  a. griffon vulture
  b. andean condor
  c. white stork
  d. humming bird
  e. angry bird

124. Little Miss Tucket sat on a bucket. What was she eating?

  a. Curds and whey.
  b. Peaches and cream.
  c. Gluten and fiber.
  d. Christmas pie.
  e. A tuna sandwich.

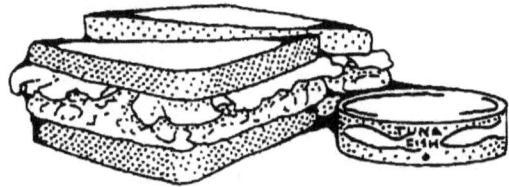

125. At the age of 255, Adwaita, died in 2006. Adwaita was a _____ .

   a. carpenter
   b. yarn spinner
   c. brick layer
   d. kick boxer
   e. tortoise

126. Ettore "Hector" Boiardi, the head caterer for President Woodrow Wilson's second marriage reception, became known as _____, after succeeding in the restaurant business and developing packaged pasta dinners for consumers to cook at home.

   a. Sidoine Benoît
   b. Bartolomeo Scappi
   c. Marcel Boulestin
   d. Madame Brassart
   e. Chef Boy-Ar-Dee

127. The Horsehead nebula is in the constellation _____ .

a. Centaurus
b. Orion
c. Scorpius
d. Ursa Major
e. Naboo

128. Water expands when it freezes because _____ .

a. it's just one of earth's mysteries
b. everything expands as it cools
c. water molecules crystalize into hexagonal structures
d. water buckets are now made of cheap plastic
e. Snow Miser wills it

129. Every two centuries, Pluto's orbit brings it closer to the sun than _____ .

   a. Neptune
   b. Saturn
   c. Jupiter
   d. Earth
   e. it can handle

130. A shark's skeleton is made of _____ .
   a. calcium carbonate
   b. mercury
   c. cartilage
   d. marrow
   e. love

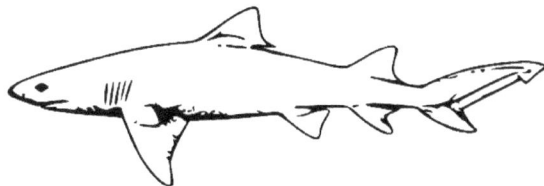

**131.** The child star of the TV sit-com "Blossom" grew up to be a neuroscientist. She was also cast on the show _____ to play one as well.

a. The X Files
b. Criminal Minds
c. Spongebob Squarepants
d. Big Bang Theory
e. Teletubbies

**132.** Which U.S. president used a wheel chair while in office?

a. Jimmy Carter
b. Franklin D. Roosevelt
c. Harry Truman
d. William Howard Taft
e. Benjamin Franklin

133. Ancient records show that the making of
_____ dates back more than 4,000 years.

  a. plastic
  b. s'mores
  c. cheese
  d. typewriters
  e. kitten mittens

134. If you dropped a hammer and a feather at the same
time while standing on the moon's surface, what would
happen?

  a. The feather would land first.
  b. The hammer and feather would float away.
  c. The hammer would land first.
  d. The hammer and feather would land at the same time.
  e. The moon would hammer in the evening, all over this
  land.

135. The continent with the smallest population is ____ .

  a. Asia
  b. North America
  c. South America
  d. Australia
  e. Antarctica

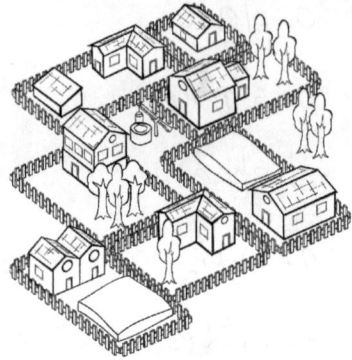

136. The faces on Mt. Rushmore are George Washington, Theodore Roosevelt, Abraham Lincoln, and ____ .

  a. Grover Cleveland
  b. Thomas Jefferson
  c. Woodrow Wilson
  d. Ulysses S. Grant
  e. Morgan Freeman

137. In Greek mythology, Artemis was known as _____ .

   a. the goddess of the hunt
   b. the goddess of the harvest
   c. the goddess of skill
   d. the goddess of music
   e. the goddess of selfies

138. Dihydrogen monoxide is a chemical name for __ .

   a. fire
   b. smoke
   c. detergent
   d. water
   e. pudding

139. Bees do not hear, but they are very sensitive to ___ .
   a. smells
   b. vibrations
   c. taste
   d. hygiene
   e. insults

140. The planet with the hottest surface temperature in our solar system is ___ .
   a. Venus
   b. Mercury
   c. Jupiter
   d. Earth
   e. Kronos

141. Human beings need the aid of _____ in order to see bacteria.

a. a magnifying glass
b. reading glasses
c. a Petri dish
d. 400x magnification
e. a strong stomach

142. In our solar system, the planet with the most gravity is _____ .

a. Pluto
b. Jupiter
c. Mars
d. Neptune
e. Dagobah

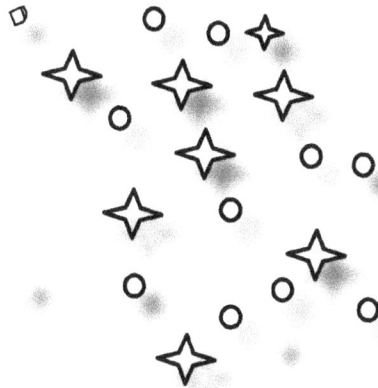

143. The "little magician" was the nickname of which president of the United States?

a. Martin Van Buren

b. Herbert Hoover

c. Bill Clinton

d. George W. Bush

e. The Amazing Mumford

144. The Turkish flag depicts which two celestial bodies?

a. The Big Dipper and Orion

b. Saturn and the full moon

c. A black hole and a meteor shower

d. Crescent Moon and Venus

e. Thor and Iron Man

145. The Erie Canal links the Great Lakes to _____.
 a. Erie, PA
 b. Panama
 c. New York City
 d. Nebraska
 e. Whoville

146. The Australian army was once called upon to help
farmers fight against _____, which were destroying crops.
 a. the British army
 b. emus
 c. fire
 d. locusts
 e. lightning storms

147. The aeolipile, invented in the first century, was a simple radial steam turbine. This technology later inspired the development of _____ .

a. jet engines
b. catapults
c. gyroscopes
d. cupcakes
e. wind powered clothes dryers

148. The name of the television show known for the phrase, "Good night, John Boy" was _____ .

a. Eight is Enough
b. The Waltons
c. Starsky and Hutch
d. General Hospital
e. Agatha Christie's Poirot

149. In 1970, fewer than 100 black bears were in the state of New Jersey. In 2010, the black bear population was _____ .

a. 3,000

b. six

c. 9 trillion

d. 798,000

e. learning to fashion complex tools

150. The energy that power plants get from flowing water is called _____ .

a. solar power

b. gushing energy

c. hydroelectric power

d. nuclear energy

e. the force

151. In 1765, the very first _____ opened in Paris. It was also the first one in the world.

   a. gym

   b. restaurant

   c. nail salon

   d. hospital

   e. video game store

152. Gelatin is made from collagen, which is extracted from ___ .

   a. aloe

   b. beans

   c. sunlight

   d. animals

   e. dreams

153. The creator of the Muppets was _____ .
   a. Shari Lewis
   b. Fred Rogers
   c. David Letterman
   d. Jim Henson
   e. Alfred E. Newman

154. Bolognese is _____ .
   a. a type of bologna sandwich
   b. a pasta sauce originating in Bologna, Italy
   c. a Saskatchewan balloon festival
   d. a breed of goats in Switzerland
   e. the language of politicians

155. Which led colonialists across the Appalachian mountains in 1775?

    a. Pioneer Trail.
    b. Trail Of Tears.
    c. Abbey Road.
    d. Wilderness Road.
    e. A tour bus.

156. The "Russian thistle" is a plant that is more commonly known as _____ .

    a. prickly pear
    b. cactus
    c. tumbleweed
    d. poison ivy
    e. Audrey II

157. The country with the most time zones is _____ .

a. France
b. Egypt
c. USA
d. Canada
e. Caspiar

158. The Emancipation Proclamation was issued by _____ .

a. Frederick Douglass
b. Julia Ward Howe
c. Abrham Lincoln
d. Simon Cameron
e. Tom Berenger

159. The first album to be released on CD was by
_____ in 1982, in Japan.
  a. Elton John
  b. Billy Joel
  c. Madonna
  d. Pink Floyd
  e. Air Supply

160. On March 21, 1965, a group of people marched from Selma to Montgomery, Alabama. This group, which grew in size to 25,000 people and marched for four days, were demanding _____ .
  a. the right for women to vote in that state.
  b. an end to segregation of public schools in that state.
  c. the right for African Americans to vote in that state.
  d. representation instead of taxation from the British Parliament.
  e. Net Neutrality

161. Troodons were dinosaurs known for their large _____ .

  a. brains
  b. ears
  c. hands
  d. tails
  e. egos

162. Flamingos are pink because _____ .

  a. their heart pumps at a rapid rate
  b. they eat a lot of pink shrimp
  c. they are covered with pink fungus
  d. they are dyed pink by their elders at birth
  e. they get embarrassed easily

163. The highest waterfall in the world, at 3,189 ft (972 m) is in _____ .

a. Canada
b. Venezuela
c. Saudi Arabia
d. Kenya
e. Ithica, NY

164. At one time, 3 nautical miles was mostly referred to as a _____ .

a. league
b. light year
c. liter
d. langley
e. lot

165. Koko, the famous gorilla who knew a modified version of American Sign Language, told her trainers that she wanted a pet _____ .

a. dog

b. cat

c. mouse

d. pony

e. human

166. The natural habitat where African lions live is the _____ .

a. jungle

b. grasslands

c. ocean

d. desert

e. Detroit

167. The city of _____ served as the temporary capital of the United States during 1790 - 1800.
   a. Boston
   b. New York
   c. Philadelphia
   d. Richmond
   e. Moscow

168. Pigeons, flamingos, and male emperor penguins are the only 3 species of birds known to produce _____ .
   a. milk
   b. live births
   c. 100 eggs per nest
   d. mating calls
   e. musicals

169. At one time, Arnold Schwarzenegger could bench press the same amount of weight as _____ .

a. two refrigerators

b. a car

c. a fully grown maple tree

d. 200 bowling balls

e. an elephant

170. The first Oscar to be awarded to an animated film was in 1991. The movie was _____ .

a. Toy Story

b. Beauty and the Beast

c. Frosty the Snowman

d. Fantasia

e. Dora the Explorer

171. An area of land that is 43,560 square feet is better known as _____.

a. a city block

b. a plot

c. an acre

d. a cul de sac

e. a walk-in shoe closet

172. The famous Shakespeare play, "Romeo and Juliet" is believed to have been written during the _____.

a. 1490's

b. 1590's

c. 1690's

d. 1790's

e. Great Depression

173. The _____'s tongue is so long, it can lick its own eyes.

   a. okapi
   b. bobcat
   c. naked mole rat
   d. desert cottontail rabbit
   e. lead singer of Kiss

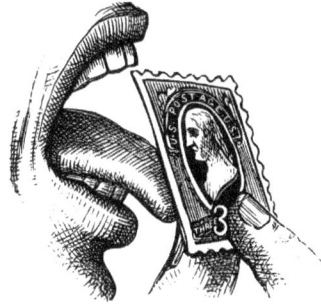

174. You can calculate the pull of _____ between two celestial objects by multiplying their mass by the square of the distance between them.

   a. velocity
   b. humidity
   c. singularity
   d. gravity
   e. tractor beams

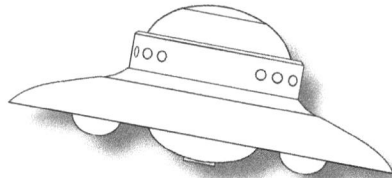

175. The Japanese word, _____ , which means "empty orchestra," has become an enjoyable, musical pastime in many countries (at least, for the participants).

a. sonata

b. piano

c. forte

d. karaoke

e. kazoo

176. On Jan. 21, 1977, his first day in office, President Jimmy Carter pardoned hundreds of thousands of ____ .

a. jay walkers

b. draft dodgers

c. tax evaders

d. counterfeiters

e. burpers

177. The United Kingdom's laws are created by the legislative body called _____ .

a. House of Elders
b. National People's Congress
c. Parliament
d. Bundestag
e. United Federation of Planets

178. Thailand shares boundaries with Cambodia, Laos, _____ and Myanmar.

a. Quebec
b. Malaysia
c. Russia
d. Vietnam
e. Oz

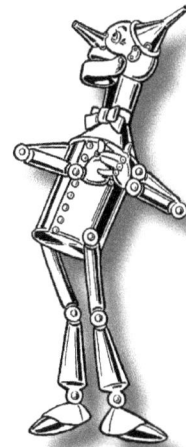

179. "Quid pro quo" is a Latin phrase that means, "_____."

    a. an equal exchange
    b. the game is tied
    c. whatever happens, happens
    d. serve one another
    e. the squid is on special

180. The longest river in the world is _____ .
    a. Mississippi
    b. Tigris
    c. Amazon
    d. Nile
    e. Moon River

181. The term "interstate highway" implies _____ .

  a. the road crosses state lines
  b. the road receives federal funding
  c. no speed limits
  d. public use is prohibited
  e. dubious rest stops

182. On April 11, 1970, three astronauts launched to go to the moon. But after a mishap en route, they had to return to earth, barely surviving the ordeal. The name of their spacecraft was _____ .

  a. Apollo 11
  b. Apollo 13
  c. Tremendous 12
  d. Soyuz
  e. Three Musketeers

183. In 1988, Nike began using its now famous slogan, "____."
    a. I'm lovin' it
    b. Save money, live better
    c. Just do it
    d. When you care enough to send the very best
    e. Let your fingers do the walking

184. The earth rotates at the speed of ____.
    a. 50 feet per hour
    b. 4,000 cycles per second
    c. 700 leagues per day
    d. 1,000 miles per hour
    e. a city bus

185. In the tall tale legends of Paul Bunyan, he worked as a _____ .

a. paper towel maker
b. lumberjack
c. steamboat builder
d. professional wrestler
e. masseuse

186. Eros was known to be the mythological god of _____ .

a. love
b. life
c. hunting
d. war
e. bananas

187. In 1972, you could buy a Pulsar -- the first
_____ for $2,100, as it was made with 18-carat
gold.

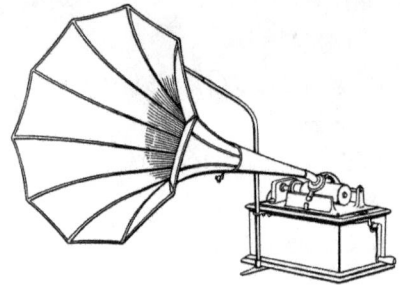

   a. digital watch

   b. remote control

   c. laptop computer

   d. mobile phone

   e. phonograph

188. Cuisine that is a fusion of both American and
Mexican food has come to be known as _____.

   a. Cajun

   b. Creole

   c. Tex-Mex

   d. Nouvelle

   e. sliders

189. _____ have stinging cells, which they use to fight each other for more undersea territory.
    a. Spider crabs
    b. Angel fish
    c. Frilled sharks
    d. Coral
    e. Scuba divers

190. Einstein's theory of general relativity includes the relationships between gravity, space, matter, speed, and _____ .
    a. distance
    b. curves
    c. time
    d. atoms
    e. carry-on luggage

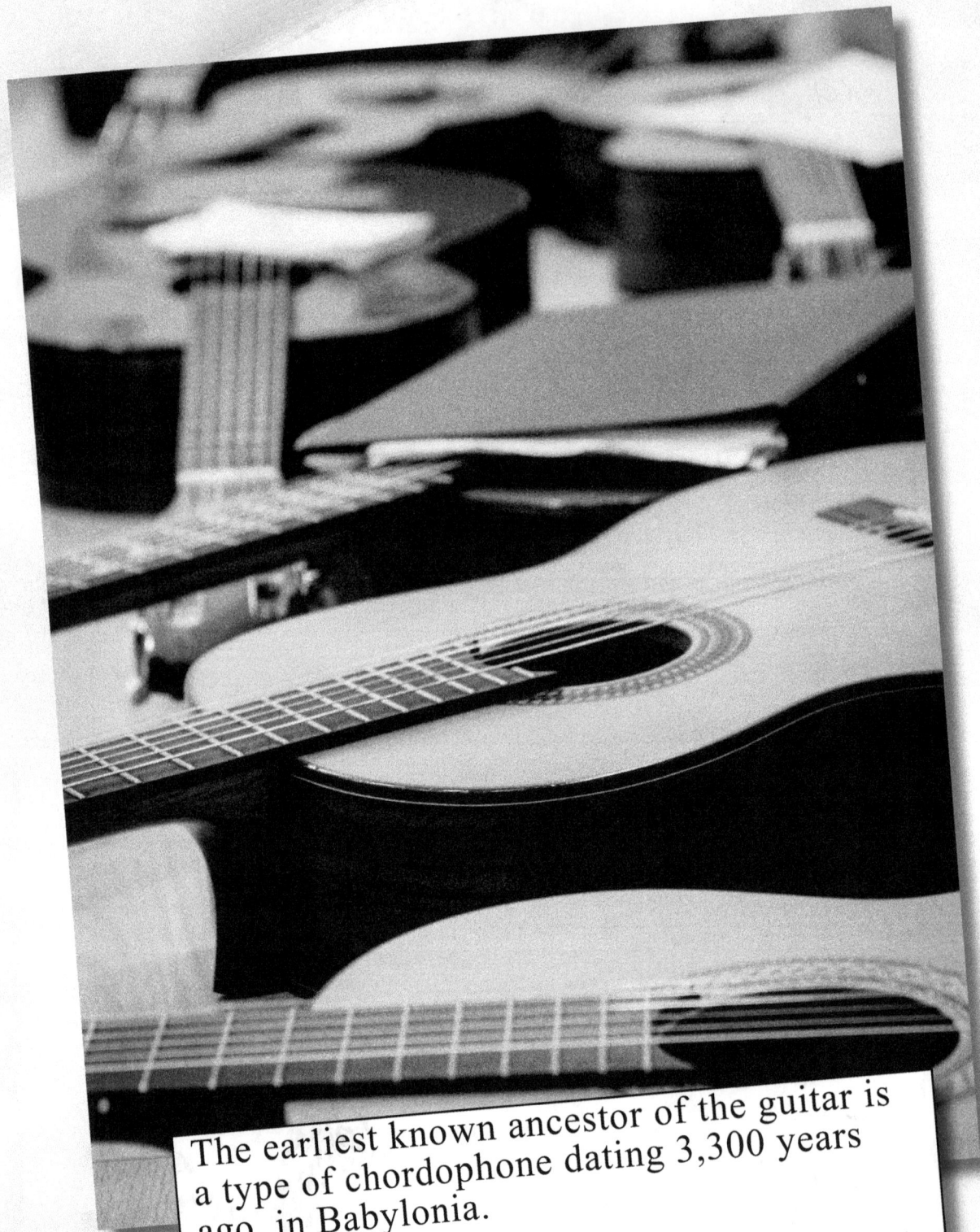

The earliest known ancestor of the guitar is a type of chordophone dating 3,300 years ago, in Babylonia.

Today, more than 2,000,000 guitars are sold each year in the United States.

# Answer Key

1.b 2.c 3.a 4.d 5.b 6.d 7.a 8.d 9.d 10.c 11.b 12.d 13.b 14.b

15.a 16.a 17.c 18.a 19.b 20.b 21.a 22.d 23.b 24.c 25.a 26.d

27.a 28.b 29.c 30.b 31.a 32.c 33.a 34.b 35.b 36.a 37.c 38.b

39.d 40.a 41.d 42.a 43.b 44.d 45.c 46.c 47.b 48.a 49.d 50.a

51.c 52.b 53.a 54.b 55.c 56.a 57.b 58.c 59.b 60.a 61.c 62.d

63.a 64.d 65.b 66.c 67.a 68.b 69.d 70.a 71.c 72.b 73.b 74.a

75.d 76.d 77.a 78.c 79.a 80.c 81.b 82.b 83.c 84.b 85.b 86.a

87.a 88.d 89.d 90.b 91.c 92.b 93.b 94.a 95.b 96.b 97.d 98.c

99.c 100.a 101.a 102.c 103.b 104.d 105.b 106.a 107.b 108.c

109.a 110.c 111.a 112.a 113.c 114.b 115.b 116.b 117.a 118.d

119.d 120.e 121.b 122.b 123.a 124.b 125.e 126.e 127.b 128.c

129.a 130.c 131.d 132.b 133.c 134.d 135.e 136.b 137.a 138.d

139.b 140.a 141.d 142.b 143.a 144.d 145.c 146.b 147.a 148.b

149.a 150.c 151.b 152.d 153.d 154.b 155.d 156.c 157.a 158.c

159.b 160.c 161.a 162.b 163.b 164.a 165.b 166.b 167.c 168.a

169.a 170.b 171.c 172.b 173.a 174.d 175.d 176.b 177.c 178.b

179.a 180.d 181.b 182.b 183.c 184.d 185.b 186.a 187.a 188.c

189.d 190.c

---

FactFrenzy.com™ Geek Scale:
171-190 answers correct = Major Nerd
152-170 answers correct = Smarty Pants
133-151 answers correct = Potentially Dangerous
132 and Under = Never Give Up. Try Again!

www.ingramcontent.com/pod-product-compliance
Lightning Source LLC
Chambersburg PA
CBHW080936040426

42443CB00015B/3435